SILVER·BURDETT

Making Music

Program Authors

Jane Beethoven
Susan Brumfield
Patricia Shehan Campbell
David N. Connors
Robert A. Duke
Judith A. Jellison

Rita Klinger
Rochelle Mann
Hunter C. March
Nan L. McDonald
Marvelene C. Moore
Mary Palmer
Konnie Saliba

Will Schmid
Carol Scott-Kassner
Mary E. Shamrock
Sandra L. Stauffer
Judith Thomas
Jill Trinka

PEARSON

Scott
Foresman

Editorial Offices: Glenview, Illinois • Parsippany, New Jersey • New York, New York
Sales Offices: Needham, Massachusetts • Duluth, Georgia • Glenview, Illinois
Coppell, Texas • Ontario, California • Mesa, Arizona

ISBN: 0-382-36569-0
2008 Edition

Contributing Authors

Audrey A. Berger
Roslyn Burrough
J. Bryan Burton
Jeffrey E. Bush
John M. Cooksey
Shelly C. Cooper
Alice-Ann Darrow
Scott Emmons
Debra Erck
Anne M. Fennell
Doug Fisher
Carroll Gonzo
Larry Harms
Martha F. Hilley
Debbie Burgoon Hines

Mary Ellen Junda
Donald Kalbach
Shirley Lacroix
Henry Leck
Sanna Longden
Glenn A. Richter
Carlos Xavier Rodriguez
Kathleen Donahue Sanz
Julie K. Scott
Gwen Spell
Barb Stevanson
Kimberly C. Walls
Jackie Wiggins
Maribeth Yoder-White

Listening Map Contributing Authors

Patricia Shehan Campbell
Jackie Chooi-Theng Lew
Ann Clements
Kay Edwards
Sheila Feay-Shaw
Kay Greenhaw

David Hebert
Hunter C. March
Carol Scott-Kassner
Mary E. Shamrock
Sandra L. Stauffer

Movement Contributing Authors

Judy Lasko
Marvelene C. Moore
Dixie Piver

Wendy Taucher
Susan Thomasson
Judith Thompson-Barthwell

Recording Producers
Buryl Red, Executive Producer

Rick Baitz
Rick Bassett
Bill and Charlene James
Joseph Joubert
Bryan Louiselle
Tom Moore
J. Douglas Pummill

Michael Rafter
Mick Rossi
Buddy Skipper
Robert Spivak
Jeanine Tesori
Linda Twine

Contents
Steps to Making Music

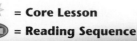
= Core Lesson
= Reading Sequence

Unit 2 Exploring Music

Unit Introduction

TE p. 42

Core Lesson =

Reading Sequence =

Learning the Language of Music TE p. 82

Unit Introduction

= Core Lesson

= Music Reading Lesson

Unit 4 Building Our Musical Skills   TE p. 122
Unit Introduction

Core Lesson = 🌟
Music Reading Lesson = 🖐

Unit 5 **Discovering New Musical Horizons** TE p. 162

Unit Introduction

⭐ = **Core Lesson**

🖐 = **Reading Sequence**

Unit 6 Making Music Our Own   TE p. 202

Unit Introduction

Core Lesson = ⭐
Music Reading Lesson = 👋

Paths to Making Music

On the Move with Loud and Soft

Move like these people or animals.

Will you move **loudly** or **softly**?

CD 1–4

Hoe Down

from *Rodeo*
by Aaron Copland

CD 1–5

Reverie

**from *Scenes from Childhood*
by Robert Schumann**

Keep It Steady

Steady beat is like your heartbeat.

Which things make a steady beat sound?

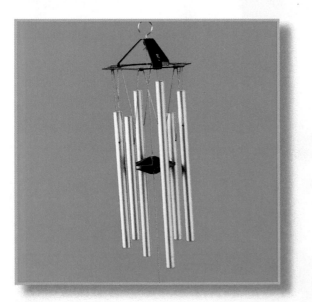

Windshield Wipers

by Mary Ann Hoberman

Windshield wipers wipe the windshield

Wipe the water off the pane

This way   That way

This way   That way

This way   That way

In the rain.

Which music has a steady beat?

CD 1–17

Watermelon Man

(excerpt) by Herbie Hancock

CD 1–18

Silver Apples of the Moon

(excerpt) by Morton Subotnick

Birthday Rhythms!

Tap the steady beat.

CD 1–27

Apples, Peaches, Pears, and Plums

Traditional Children's Rhyme

Ap-ples,   peach-es,   pears, and   plums.

Tell me   when your   birth-day   comes.

Rhythm is the pattern of the words.

Clap the rhythm of the words.

Ap-ples,   peach-es,   pears, and   plums.

Tell me   when your   birth-day   comes.

High and Low

CD 1–35
MIDI 2

The Little Green Frog
Traditional Song from the United States

Listen to the song.

When does the **melody** leap high?

lump!

Ga-

Move like the little green frog.

Frogs like to leap in lily ponds!

 **Connection**

▲ *White Water Lilies*
by Claude Monet
(1840–1926)

Listen for high and
low sounds.

CD 1–37

Andante quieto

from *Three Nocturnes for Piano Trio*
by Ernest Bloch

9

Leaves Dance UP and Down

Follow the leaves as you sing.

All the leaves are fall - ing down,

Fall - ing gent - ly to the ground,

CD 1–38

Leaves

Words and Music by Arvida Steen

When does the wind lift the leaves **up** ?

Now the wind will lift them high,

Lift them gent - ly to the sky.

My Voice

We can use our voices in different ways.

Look at each picture to the right.

How are the children using their voices?

CD 1–57
MIDI 3
Sing! Speak! Whisper! Shout!

Words and Music by Rick Bassett

Sing!

Speak!

Whisper!

Shout!

13

Fast or Slow?

Expression

CD 2–15

Freight Train
Words and Music by E. Cotton

What can move **fast?**

What can move **slow?**

How can you **move** fast?

How can you **move** slow?

Rainy Day Rhythm

Sing the song.

Tap each umbrella on the steady beat.

Clap the rhythm of the words.

Rain,   rain,   go   a   -   way,

Come a - gain some oth - er   day.

Read the rhythm.

CD 2–27 **Rain, Rain**
Traditional Children's Song

Rain,   rain,   go   a - way.

Come   a - gain   some   oth - er   day.

17

Answer the Call!

When someone calls, you answer.

Pat on the **call.**

Clap on the **response.**

CD 2–33

Shortnin' Bread

African American Folk Song

call   response

Shortnin' Bread

I do love

I do love

Mama loves

Papa loves

Everybody loves

Create your own response.

Sailing High and Low

Charlie's boat sails up and down.

Sing the song and follow his boat.

Point to each boat on the beat.

The melody goes high and low.

Charlie over the Water
Traditional Song from the United States

Charlie over the wa - ter,

Charlie over the sea._____

Charlie caught a big fish, but

Charlie couldn't catch me._____

What Makes That Sound?

What do you see in the pictures?

Listen to the sounds.

What makes each sound?

CD 2–54
Junk Music Montage

COOKIES

I can make sounds, too!

23

Clap, Tap, and Pat

People create music in different ways.

They can sing and play instruments.

People can also clap, tap, pat, and stamp.

▲ Maori *poi* ball dancers

CD 2–55

Toia mai te waka
Maori Folk Song from New Zealand

Move on the steady beat of the song.

Paddle the canoe.

M·U·S·I·C M·A·K·E·R·S

Kiri Te Kanawa

Kiri Te Kanawa is a famous singer.
She is from New Zealand.

CD 2–59
Piki mai
**Maori Welcome Song
from New Zealand**

Soft Pops Loud Pops

CD 3–1

We're Making Popcorn
by Judith Thomas

Old-fashioned popcorn was made in a pan.

Pop

Pop

Listen to the music.

When is the sound soft?

When is it the loudest?

Pop Pop Popcorn

Planting Long and Short Sounds

Rice is grown all over the world.

People grow rice in many different ways.

Cha yang wu (Rice Planting Song)

Folk Song from China

Sing the song.

Read and **clap** this rhythm pattern.

Hai hai   huh,   hai hai   ho,

Plant-ing   rice is   ver-y   nice.

Soccer Sounds and Silences

Pretend you are a soccer player.

Listen to the music.

Dribble the ball and **move** on the beat.

Stop the ball on the silent beat.

CD 3–19

¡Viva el fútbol!
(I Love Soccer!)

Words and Music by Moretto and Bassett

Soc-cer   is my   game.

It's the   best by   far.

31

Same or Different?

CD 3–31

The Rain Sings a Song

Words and Music by Irving Lowens

Sing a song about rain.

What parts of the song are the same?

What parts are different?

Play this pattern as you sing.

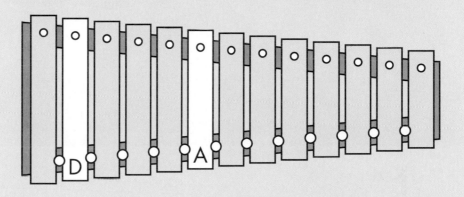

Create an accompaniment for the song.

Meet so and mi

CD 3–36

Star Light, Star Bright
Traditional Song from the United States

Sing and point to the stars.

High and low sounds have musical names.

Read *so* and *mi* on the staff.

so

so   mi   so   mi

This artist used swirls of color in his painting.

𝒜rts Connection

▲ *Starry Night* (1889)
by Vincent van Gogh

so

mi

Timbre

Thump, Rattle, and Scrape

Listen to these instruments.

How is each one played?

Tabla ▶

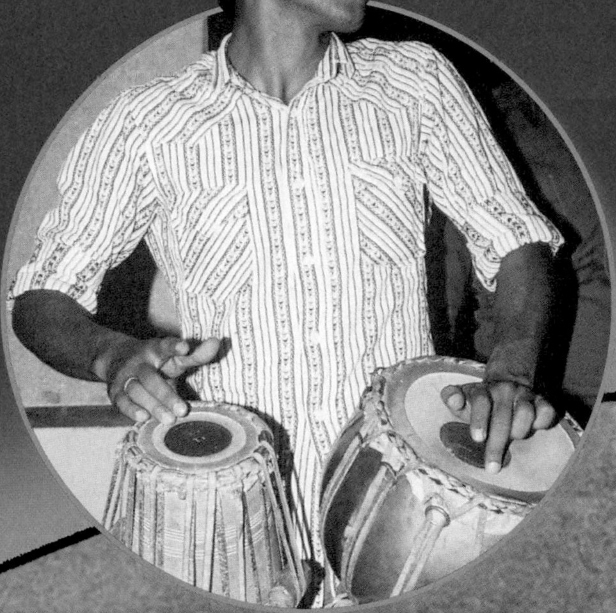

Shekere ▼

Djembe ▲

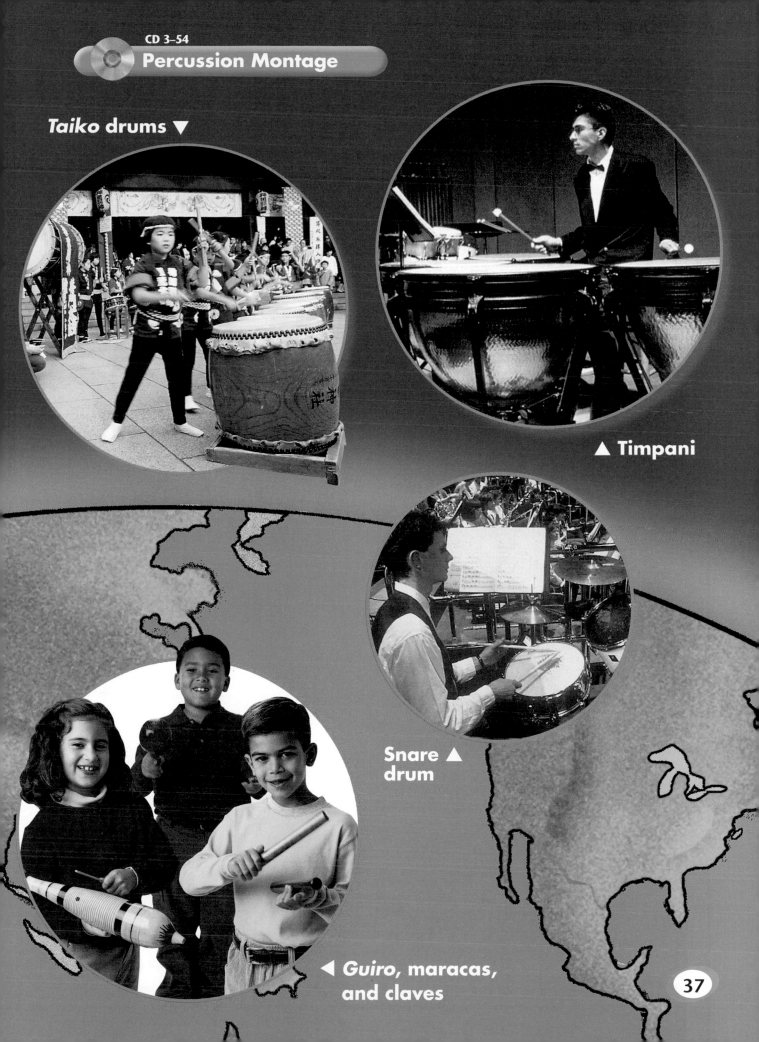

Percussion Montage

Taiko drums ▼

▲ Timpani

Snare ▲
drum

◀ *Guiro, maracas,*
and claves

37

Faster, Faster, Stop!

Change the **tempo** as you say the poem.

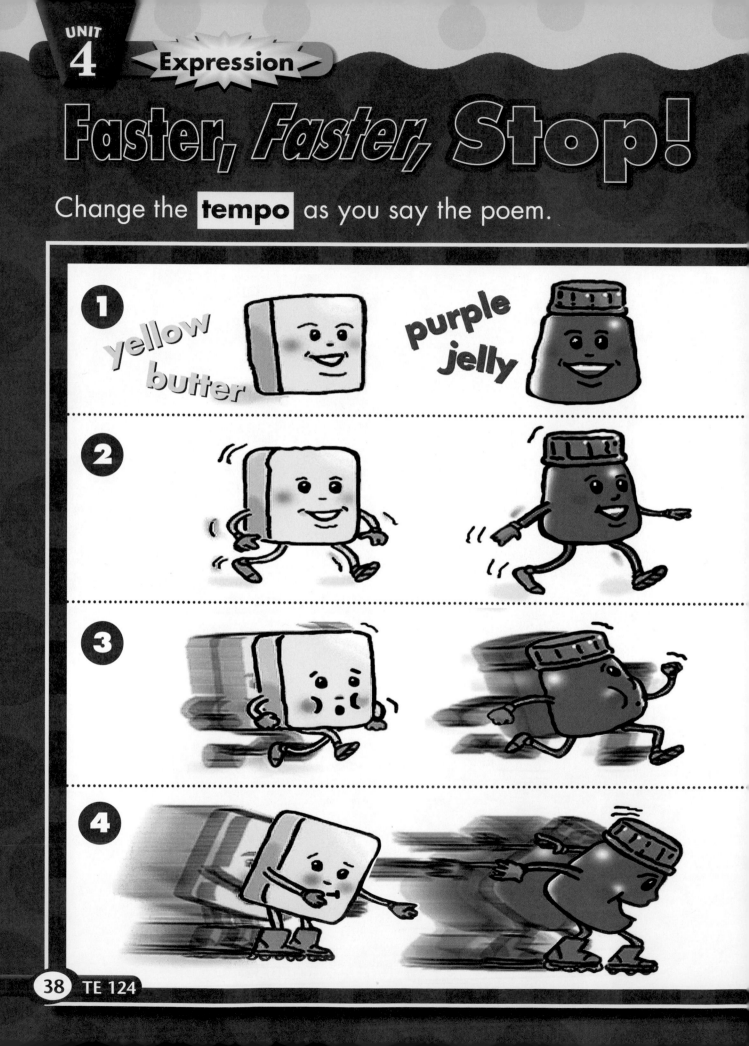

Cat at Rest

A **rest** is a beat with no sound.

Read and **clap** the rhythms.

Arts Connection

▲ Cat on a
Yellow Pillow
by Franz Marc
(1880–1916)

Verse and Refrain

This song has two sections.

It has a **verse** **and a** **refrain.**

CD 4–35

Nampaya omame

(There Come Our Mothers)

Traditional Zulu Song from South Africa

Rock forward and back on the verse.

Rock from side to side on the refrain.

Form

Two Different Sections

This song has two different sections.

Call the first section **A**.

Call the second section **B**.

CD 4-43

Amefuri (Japanese Rain Song)
School Song from Japan

Play the steady beat on a 🥁 in section A.

Play the rhythm on 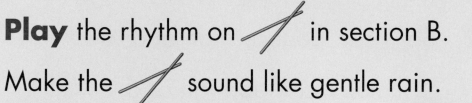 in section B.

Make the 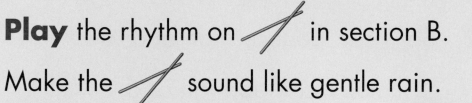 sound like gentle rain.

B

Bounce to a New Note

Balls can bounce high and low.

A melody can go high and low.

Bounce High, Bounce Low

Traditional Game Song from the United States

Listen for the *so* and *mi* pitch patterns in this song.

so   ?   so   mi

so so   ? ?   so   mi

The new pitch is *la*.

so   la   so   mi

so so   la la   so   mi

CD 5–1

Chang
(Elephant)
Folk Song from Thailand

Instrument Sounds

Music is a part of celebrations everywhere.

In Thailand there is a celebration for elephants.

Listen to this song about elephants.

These instruments are
from Thailand.

How are they played?

Getting Louder, Getting Softer

Listen! A band is far away.

Clap the beat.

CD 5–26

The Parade Came Marching
Words and Music by John Forster

Listen for the loud and soft

parts in this famous march.

CD 5–28

The Stars and Stripes Forever

by John Philip Sousa

51

Woof, Woof, Woof! A Pattern

Even a dog's bark can create patterns.

Say this pattern.

Woof!   Woof!   Woof! Woof! Woof!

The farmer had a dog named Bingo.

Help spell Bingo's name as you **sing**.

CD 5–29

Bingo

Folk Song from the United States

B,   I,   N, G, O

Clap Bingo's **pattern** when you hear it.

The farmer just loves his dog.

Help him show Bingo how he feels.

Clap where you see hands.

	I		N	G	O
			N	G	O
				G	O
					O

Will you **clap** or **play**
Bingo's pattern as you sing?

Beats in Two

Beats can be grouped in sets of 2.

The first beat is the strong beat.

Play your cymbals on the strong beat.

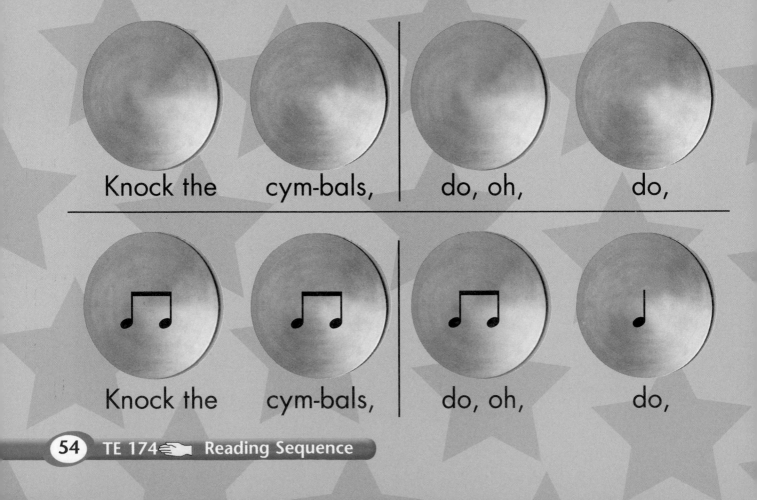

Knock the   cym-bals, | do, oh,   do,

Knock the   cym-bals, | do, oh,   do,

Knock the Cymbals
Play-Party Game from Texas

This song is written in meter in 2.

Knock the cym - bals, do, oh, do,

Knock the cym - bals, do, oh, do,

Knock the cym - bals, do, oh, do,

Hel - lo, Su - san Brown - o.

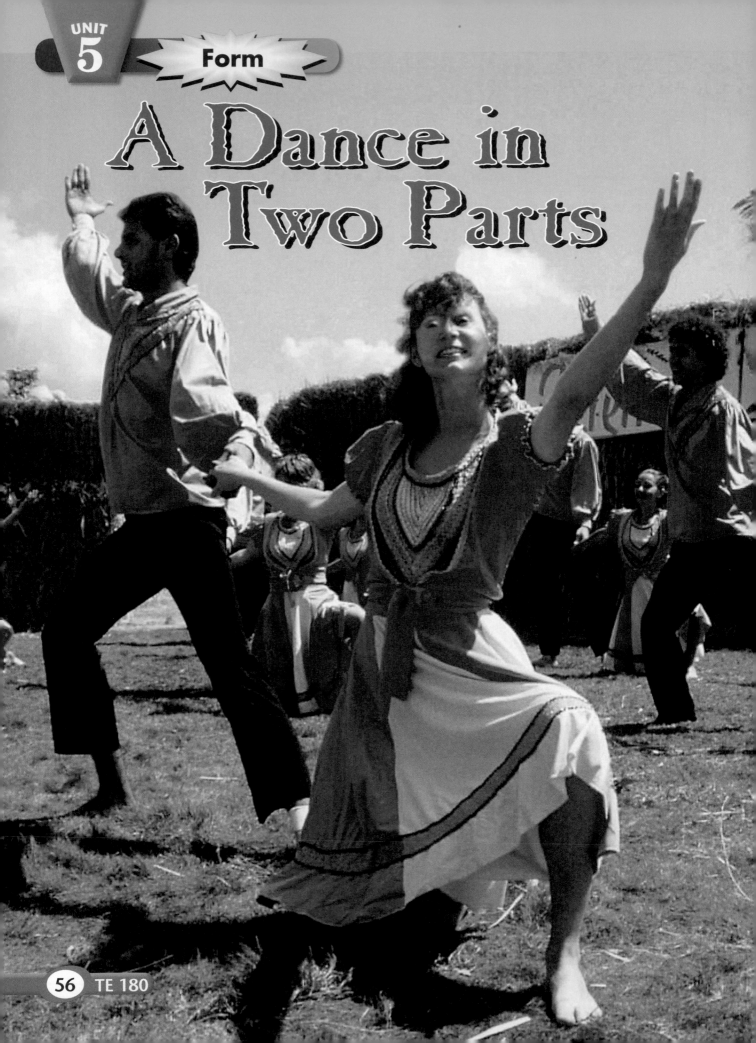

A Dance in Two Parts

Yesh lanu taish (We Have a Goat)
Folk Song from Israel

Sing this song about a goat.

It is a folk dance from Israel.

How will you **move** on the verse?

How will you **move** on the refrain?

More *so*, *mi*, and *la*

CD 6–17

Snail, Snail
Traditional Children's Song

Follow the snails.

Read the pitches.

so | 2/4 | so mi so mi

so so la la so so mi

CD 6–22

Lemonade
Children's Game Song

so **2/4**

Here we come.

Where from?

New York.

What's your trade?

Lem - on - ade.

Give us some, don't be a - fraid.

59

Timbre

Ding! Dong! Bong!

Musical instruments have their own special sounds.

Listen to these instruments.

CD 6–29

Hard Times

by Len "Boogsie" Sharpe

Where might you hear
this instrument being played? ▶

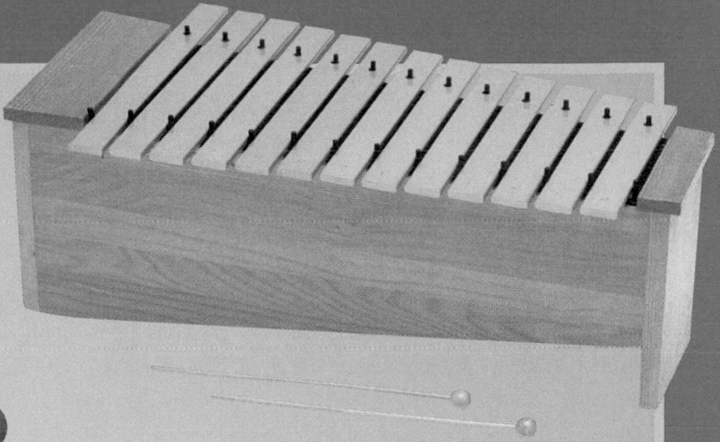

CD 6–30
Sekar jepun
**Traditional Balinese Kebyar
Gamelan Music**

Fast or Slow?
Loud or Soft?

CD 6–41

Hungarian Dance No. 3
by Johannes Brahms

Listen for three sections in this music.

1

Miguel Harth-Bedoya

Conductors lead orchestras, bands, and choirs.

Miguel Harth-Bedoya is the conductor of the Fort Worth Symphony Orchestra.

He helps the musicians know when to play loud or soft, fast or slow.

How is each one different?

2

3

Rhythm

Rug Bug Rhythms

CD 7–1

Little Black Bug

Words by Margaret Wise Brown
Music by Ruth Boshkoff

Read the rhythm patterns.

Play them on a 🥁 or a △ .

Lit - tle   black   bug,

Bug,   ugh,   ugh.

Create your own patterns using

♩ , ♫ , and 𝄾 .

Arts **Connection**

cuna Indian Molas from
the San Blas Islands ▶

65

Moving

Same Different Same

CD 7–11

B-A, Bay

Folk Song from the United States

Listen for the different sections in this song.

How many sections do you hear?

A

Pat and **clap** in section **A**.

Move to show the different sections.

B
Elbow swing your partner in section **B**.

Move with Mouse on so, la, and mi

Sing "Hickory, Dickory, Dock" as the **A** section.

Use *so*, *mi*, and *la* as the pitches.

CD 7–16

Hickory, Dickory, Dock

Mother Goose Rhyme

Melody and Arrangement by Julie Scott

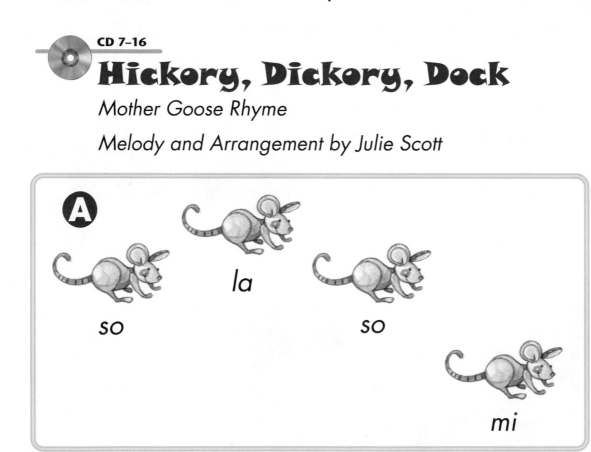

A

la

so   so

mi

Tap the steady beat with the **B** section.

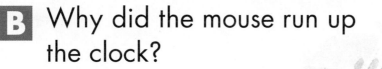

B Why did the mouse run up the clock?

Because she was living there.

Why did the mouse run down the clock?

The sound gave her a scare!

69

Look Out Below, Here Comes do!

Sing the song "Apple Tree."

Use pitch names *so*, *mi*, and *la*.

Apple Tree

CD 7–23

Traditional Song from the United States

Ap - ple tree, ap - ple tree,

Will your ap - ples fall on me?

I won't cry and I won't shout,

If your ap - ple knocks me out.

Hum the new note.

Is it higher or lower than *so*?

Is it higher or lower than *mi*?

The new note is called *do*.

Xylobone or Xylophone?

Create an accompaniment for this poem about fossils.

Play your accompaniment on a [xylophone].

CD 7–30

Mammoth (poem)

by Richard Edwards

Mammoth

(excerpt)

by Richard Edwards

Once I waved my wild tusks high,

Once I was colossal,

Now I never see the sky,

Now I'm just a fossil.

Some musical instruments are made of wood.

Listen for the xylophone in this music.

What other instruments do you hear?

CD 7–31
Fossils

from *Carnival of the Animals*
by Camille Saint-Saëns

Fossils Listening Map

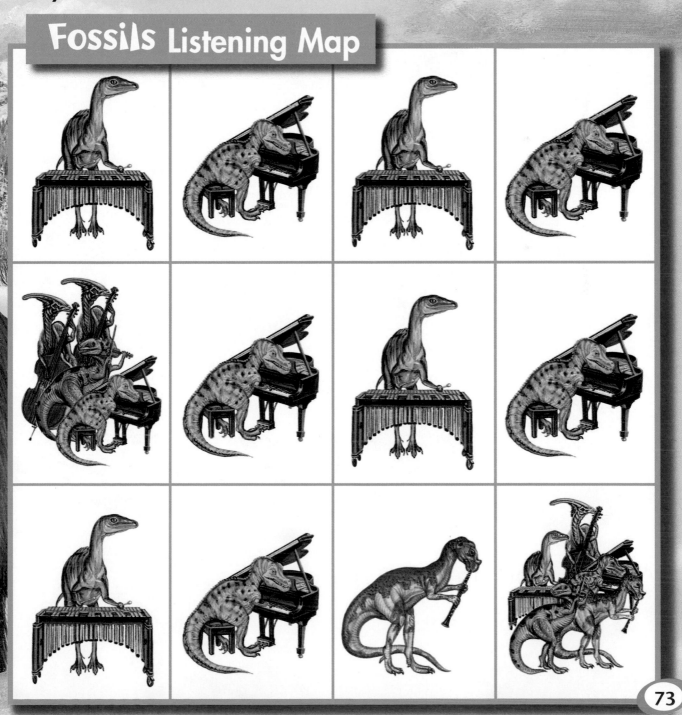

Ant Antics

CD 8–1

The Ants Go Marching

Words Adapted by Edith Fowke
Music by Patrick S. Gilmore

1 one

2 two

3 three

4 four

5 five

6 six

We sing counting songs at school.

Pat the steady beat.

Meet the Instruments

CD 8–12

The Little Red Hen
by Judith Thomas

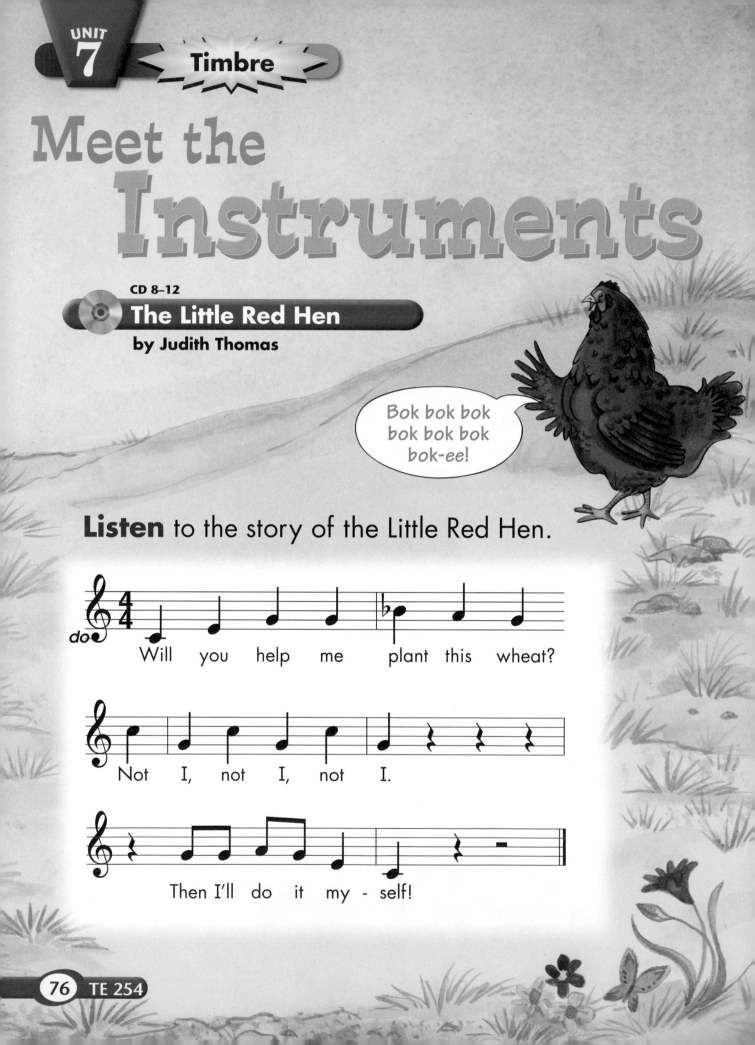

Bok bok bok bok bok bok bok-ee!

Listen to the story of the Little Red Hen.

Will you help me plant this wheat?

Not I, not I, not I.

Then I'll do it my-self!

Someday you might play in a school orchestra.

Here are some instruments you might play.

Listen for the special sound of each instrument.

The Little Red Hen Listening Map

Moving

Sing and Spell

Sing this song and spell the words.
What other words can you spell?

__og

__an

__op

c_at

CD 8–30

I Can't Spell Hippopotamus
Words and Music by J. Fred Coots

hat   **cat**   **fat**

dog   **log**   **hog**

top   **hop**   **mop**

ban   **man**   **fan**

Look, Listen...
Lullaby

Look at this statue.

How does this statue
make you feel?

Arts Connection

◀ *Hush-a-bye Baby*
by Aimé-Jules Dalou
(1838–1902)

A little girl rocks her toy elephant to sleep.

Listen for this melody in the music.

CD 8–34

Jimbo's Lullaby

from *Children's Corner Suite*
by Claude Debussy

Jimbo's Lullaby
Listening Map

We Sing About
Our Country

Sing a song about America.

Listen for words that name places.

CD 9–1

This Land Is Your Land

(Refrain only)
Words and Music by Woody Guthrie

This land is your land,

This land is my land,

From California to the New York Island;

From the redwood forest

To the Gulf Stream waters;

This land was made for you and me.

CD 9–3

You're a Grand Old Flag

by George M. Cohan

Families Around the World

You are an important member of a family.

How are families alike?

How are they different?

Sing this song about families.

Play this rhythm pattern on 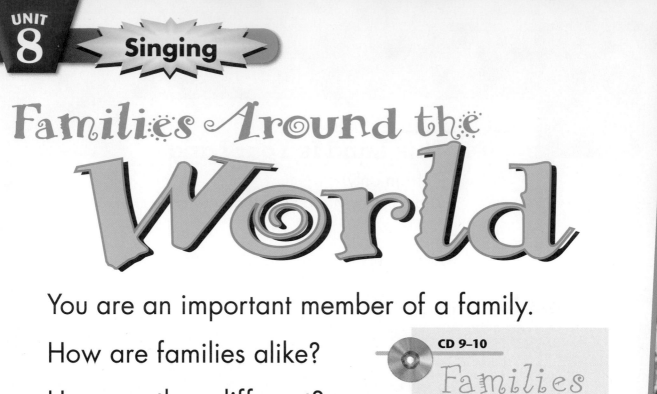 or a △.

CD 9–10

Families
Words and Music
by James A. Forbes, Jr.

‖: ♩   𝄾   𝄾   𝄾 :‖

Moving

A Bump-a-Deedle Dance

How do you do the Bump-a-Deedle dance?

How many ways can you **move?**

Create your own Bump-a-Deedle dance.

CD 9–15

Everybody Says

Words and Music by Malvina Reynolds

Ev - ery - bo - dy bump a dee - dle dance with me.

Alvin Ailey

American Dance Theater

These dancers perform all over the world.
They move to different kinds of music.
They create many shapes with their bodies.

My Family and Me

87

Families Work and Sing Together

This family lives in Peru.

How can families work together?

CD 9–24

Los maizales
(The Cornfields)
Folk Song from Peru

Music can have layers of sound.

Listen to this music from Peru.

What instruments do you hear?

Tema de maimara **Listening Map**

1

2

3

4

5

CD 9–28

Tema de maimara
Traditional Andean

Singing in the Tub

Bath time can be fun.

Some people sing in the bath.

Sing this bath time song.

Follow the pictures.

1

CD 9–39
Scrub-a Dub
by David Eddleman

Glub-a glub!

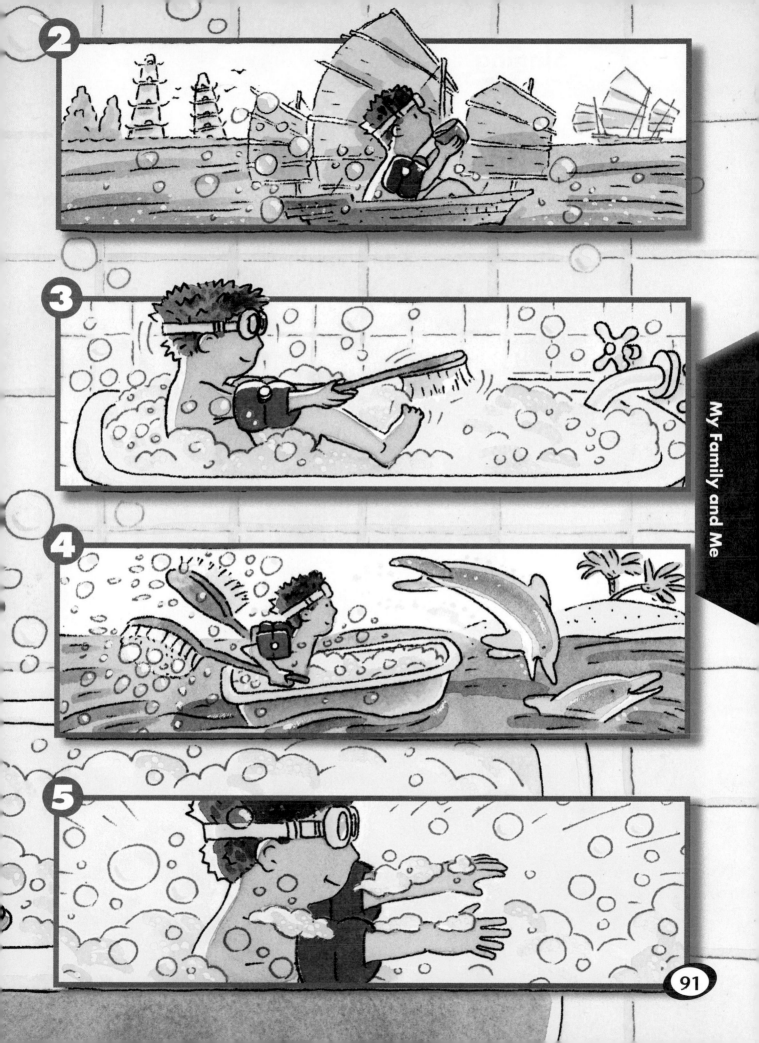

Singing

How Do You Sing Hello?

People say *hello* in many ways.

Sorida

Game Song from the Shona People of Zimbabwe

Sing and **move** to *"Sorida."*

How can you say *hello* without using words?

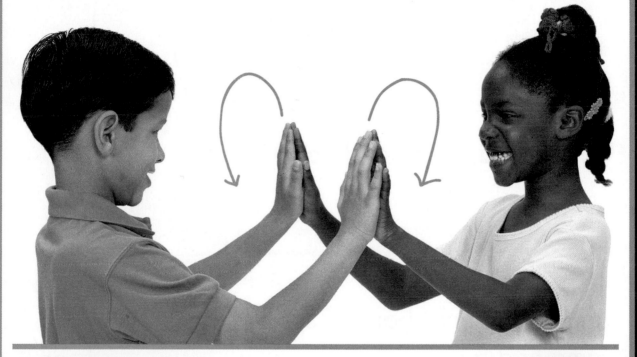

Adventures with Friends

93

musical GAMES

Sing and say this jump rope rhyme.

Pat and **clap** the steady beat.

CD 10–11

Banana Splits (speech piece)

Jump-rope Rhyme

Banana, banana, banana splits,
Mama had a baby chick.
Chick was a hen,
Do it over again,
Banana, banana, banana splits.

Green, Green, Rocky
African American Singing Game

Listen to "Green, Green, Rocky."

Find this pattern in the song.

do   Rock - y

Friends Make Music

This poem tells about being a friend.

How to Be a Friend
by Pat Lowery Collins

Keep a secret
Tell a wish
Listen
to
a dream

Create an **A** **B** **A** form.

The poem is the **A** section.

Create a **B** section using instruments.

Arts **Connection**

▶ *Patticake* (1986)
by Brenda Joysmith

Listen for special sounds in the song.

Create sound effects to accompany the song.

Two by Two

Sing this song about animals.

How are the animals walking?

Play a walking sound on the drum.

CD 11–1

Noah's Shanty

Words and Music by Malcolm Abbs

Play this accompaniment.

UNIT 10 — Moving

A Mouse At Home

What does Mouse like to do at home?

Move like Mouse as you **sing** the song.

CD 11–7

The Little Mouse

Words and Music by Bill Meek

Tap on the strong beats.

Sniff!	Sniff!	Sniff!	Sniff!
I	smell	cheese.	

Play the strong beats as you sing the song.

Creating

Sea Treasures

Say this speech piece.

Pat and **clap** the steady beat.

CD 11–9

Beach Rap

Words and Music
by Judith Thomas

Going on a shell walk,
Grand sandy beach,
Looking for the treasures
That are in my reach!

lightning
whelk

sand dollar

pink conch

cockle
shell

Create rhythm patterns with shell names.

Play the patterns on instruments.

purple
scallop

alphabet
cone

worm shell

baby's ear
moon

auger shell

105

Form

A Flutter of Butterflies

Sing the song. Which parts are alike?

CD 11–21

Ah! Les jolis papillons

(Ah! The Pretty Butterflies)

Folk Song from St. Pierre and Miquelon

Each winter, monarch butterflies fly to Mexico.

✐Arts Connection

▲ *Untitled* (1997)
by Bob Marstall

Listen for the fluttering sounds of butterflies in this music.

CD 11–27
Butterfly
by Edvard Grieg

A Spring Dance

Winters in Russia are long.

Russian people celebrate when spring comes.

They dance and sing songs about growing things.

CD 12–1
MIDI 15

Khorovod (Round Dance)

Folk Song from Russia

Follow the directions and **move** to the music.

Speaking of Treats...

Is hot chocolate one of your favorite treats?

Some children stir the chocolate with a special beater—a *molinollo*.

CD 12–7

El Chocolate (Chocolate)

Children's Rhyme from Mexico
English Words and Music by José-Luis Orozco

Sing the pattern as you stir the chocolate.

cho - co - la - te, cho - co -

la - te

What are your favorite treats?

Create rhythm patterns with treat names.

1. can - dy   ap - ples

2. pop - corn   pop-ping

Say your patterns
to tell a tale of treats.

Sing Me a Story

Sing this story song.

How does the story end?

 CD 12–17

I Know an Old Lady

Words by Rose Bonne
Music by Alan Mills

Who is in every verse?

Create animal sounds for each verse.

113

Movin' On with a Silly Song

What do you think this song is about?

Sing this silly song.

CD 12–24

Hi Heidi Ho

*Words and Music
by Lucille Panabaker*

Play these rhythm patterns.

Make up a funny walk.

Teach it to a friend.

115

Musical Journey to Jupiter

Let's take a musical trip to the planet Jupiter.

Jupiter is the largest planet in our solar system.

CD 13–4

Jupiter

from *The Planets*
by Gustav Holst

Listen to this music about Jupiter.

What happens to the tempo?

What instruments do you hear?

MUSIC MAKERS

Gustau Holst

Gustav Holst (1874–1934) was a composer.
He loved to study about the stars and planets.
He wrote music about the planets.

Play a Birthday Pattern

Which pattern will you **play?**

1.

2.

Which instrument will you use?

hand drum   **tambourine**   **rhythm sticks**

The End

by A. A. Milne

When I was One,
I had just begun.

When I was Two,
I was nearly new.

When I was Three,
I was hardly me.

When I was Four,
I was not much more.

When I was Five,
I was just alive,

But now I am Six, I'm clever as clever.
So I think I'll be Six for ever and ever.

CD 13–8

The End (poem)

by A. A. Milne

Sing to Celebrate

Candles and lights are part of many celebrations.

Songs tell why each holiday is special.

Sing on these special days.

A Patriotic Song

Sing this special song about our country.

Follow the direction of the melody.

14–27

America

Words by Samuel Francis Smith   *Traditional Melody*

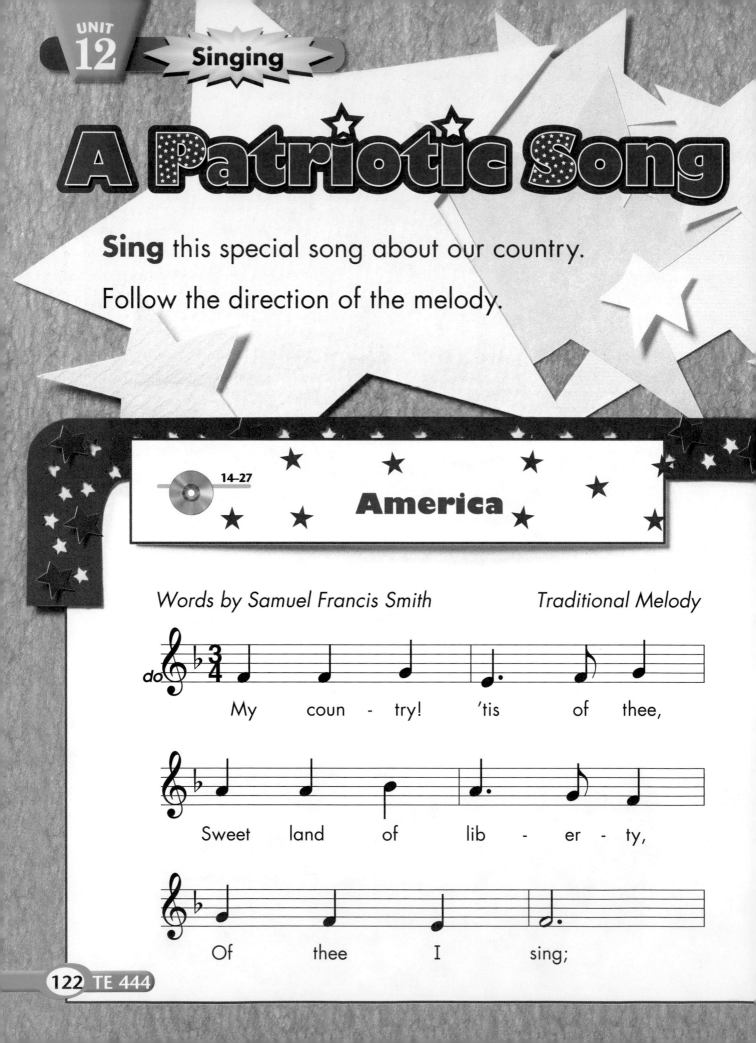

My   coun - try!   'tis   of   thee,

Sweet   land   of   lib - er - ty,

Of   thee   I   sing;

Reading Sequence 1, TE page 10

CD 1–14
MIDI 18

Rhythm: Reading Steady Beat

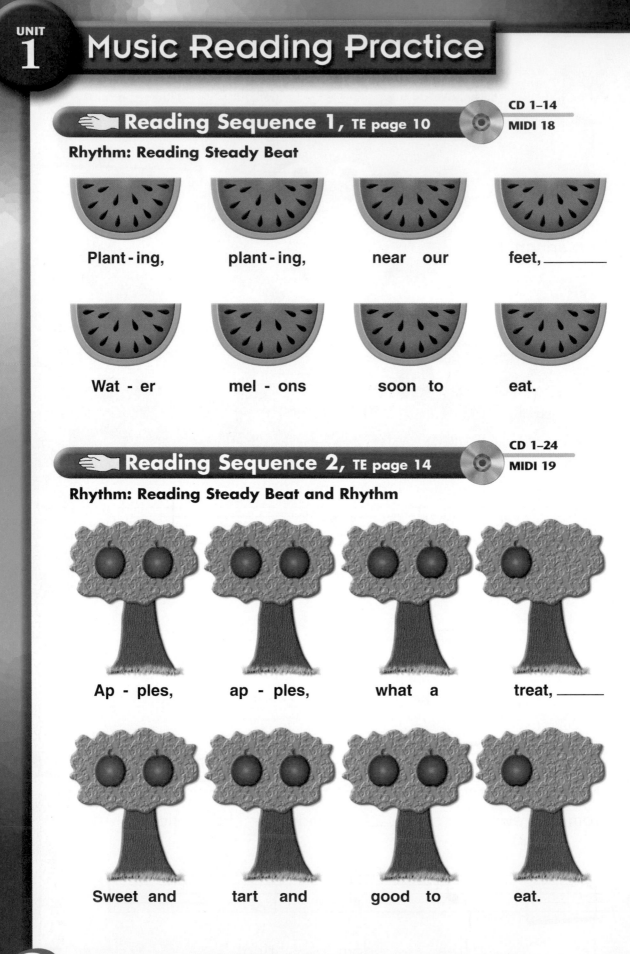

Plant - ing, plant - ing, near our feet, _____

Wat - er mel - ons soon to eat.

Reading Sequence 2, TE page 14

CD 1–24
MIDI 19

Rhythm: Reading Steady Beat and Rhythm

Ap - ples, ap - ples, what a treat, _____

Sweet and tart and good to eat.

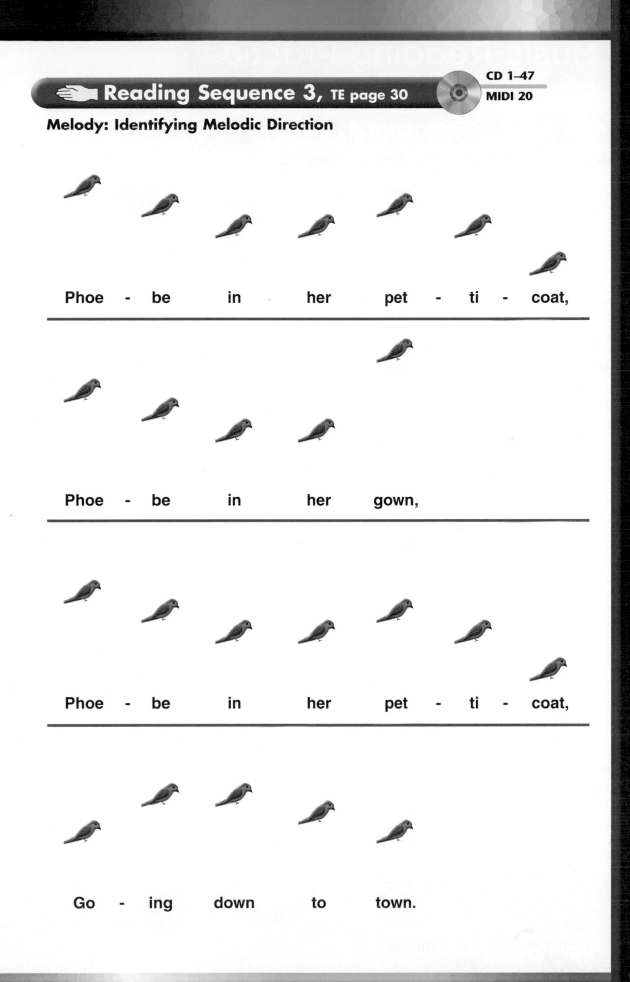

Melody: Identifying Melodic Direction

Phoe - be in her pet - ti - coat,

Phoe - be in her gown,

Phoe - be in her pet - ti - coat,

Go - ing down to town.

Music Reading Practice

Reading Sequence 4, TE page 32

Melody: Same or Different Melodic Patterns

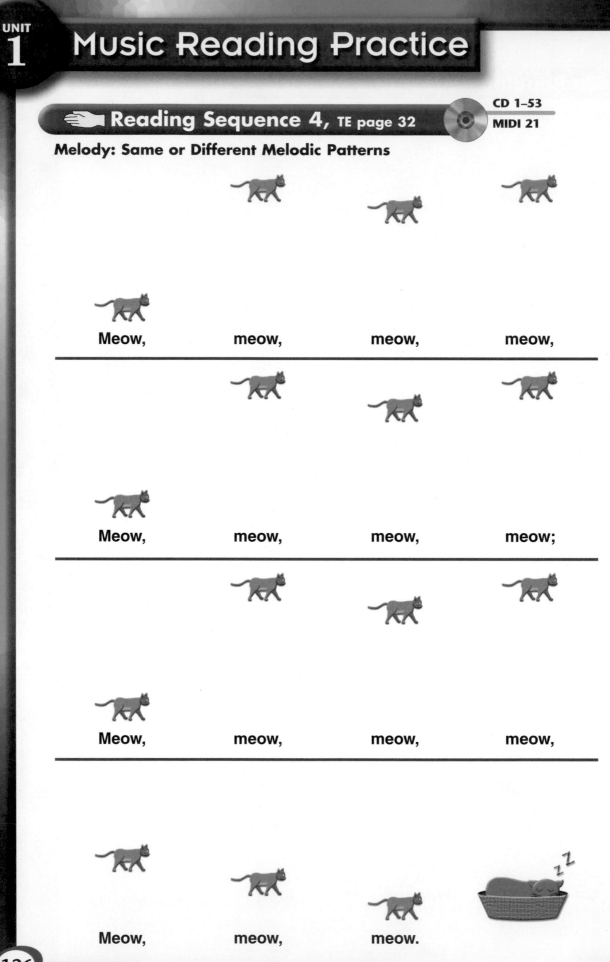

Meow,   meow,   meow,   meow,

Meow,   meow,   meow,   meow;

Meow,   meow,   meow,   meow,

Meow,   meow,   meow.

Reading Sequence 5, TE page 50

CD 2–25
MIDI 22

Rhythm: Reading Beat and Rhythm

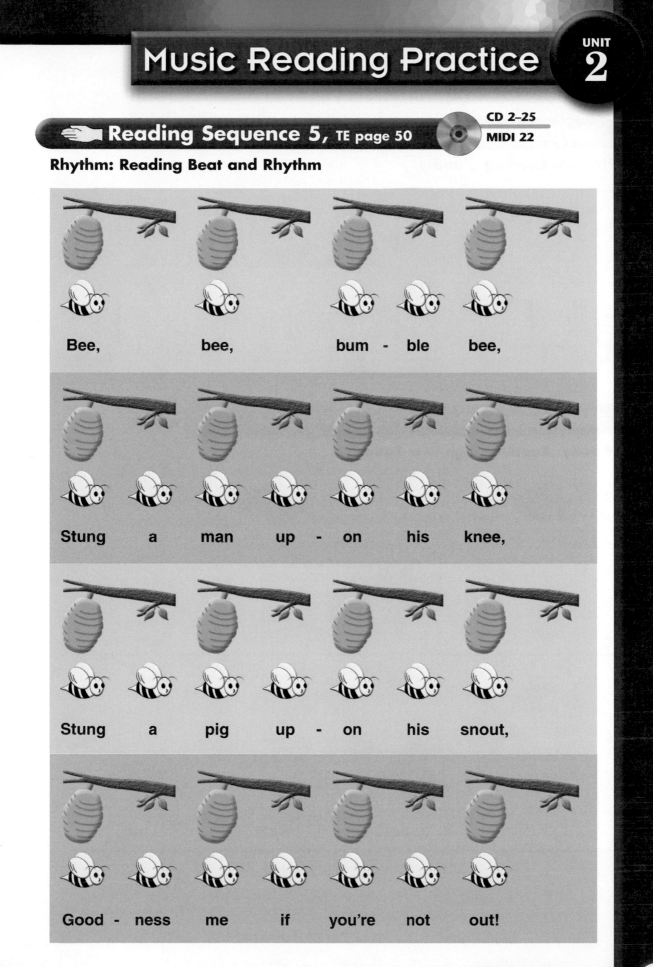

Bee,　　bee,　　bum - ble　bee,

Stung　a　man　up - on　his　knee,

Stung　a　pig　up - on　his　snout,

Good - ness　me　if　you're　not　out!

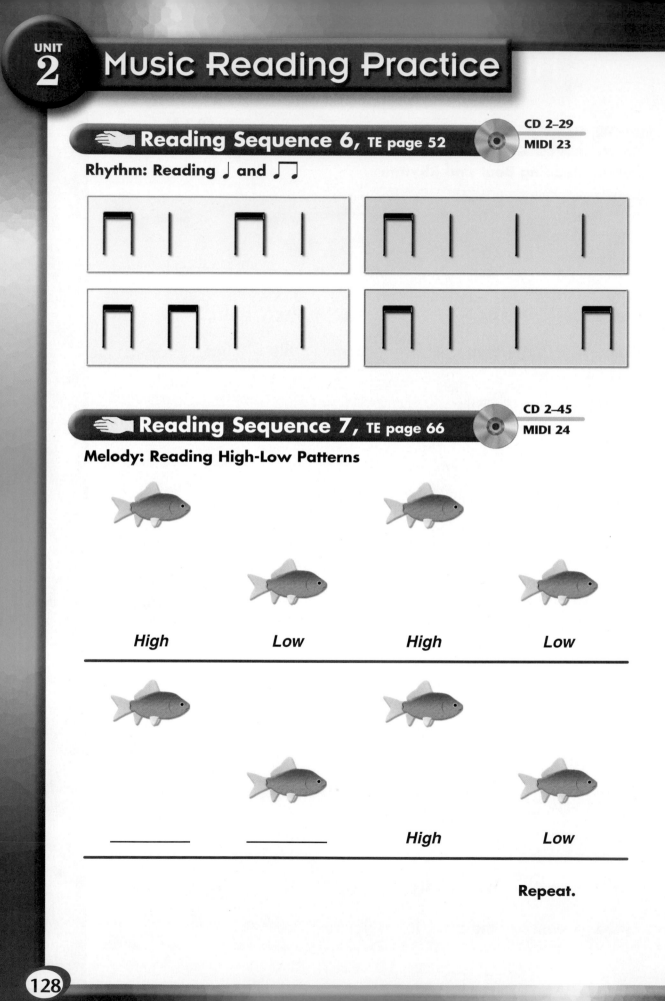

CD 2–51
MIDI 25

Melody: Reading High-Low Patterns

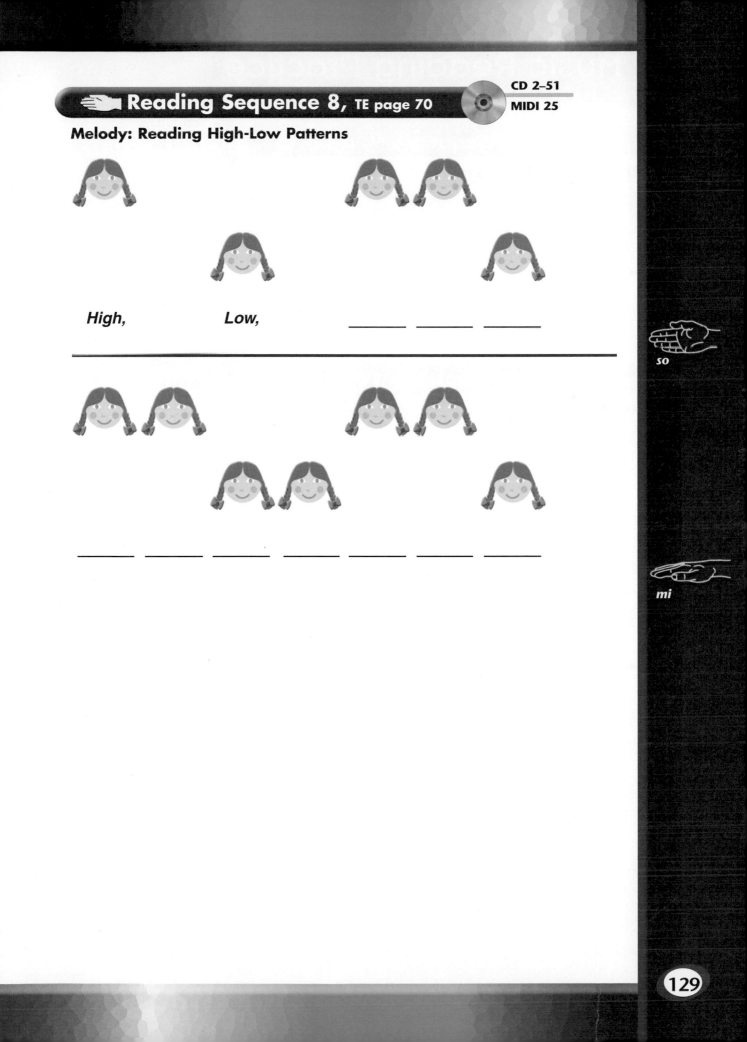

High,   Low,   _____ _____ _____

_____ _____ _____ _____ _____ _____ _____

so

mi

129

Music Reading Practice

Reading Sequence 9, TE page 88

CD 3–9
MIDI 26

Rhythm: Reading ♩ and ♫

Reading Sequence 10, TE page 98

CD 3–28
MIDI 27

Rhythm: Reading ♩ and ♫; Preparing 𝄽

Melody: Reading *so* and *mi*

so   mi   so   mi

so

so   so   mi   mi   so   so   mi

so   so   mi   mi   so   so   mi

so

mi

CD 3–46
MIDI 29

Reading Sequence 12, TE page 110

Melody: Reading *so* and *mi*

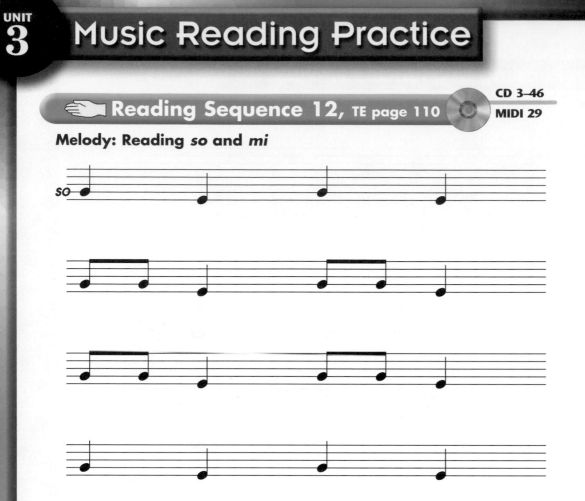

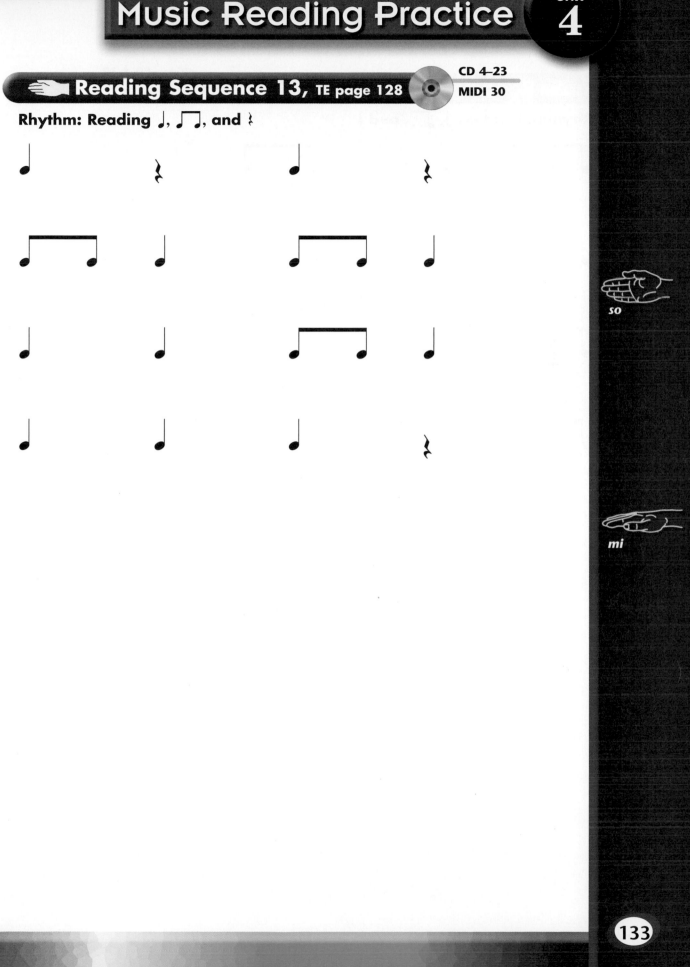

Reading Sequence 14, TE page 134

CD 4–32
MIDI 31

Rhythm: Reading ♩, ♫, **and** 𝄾

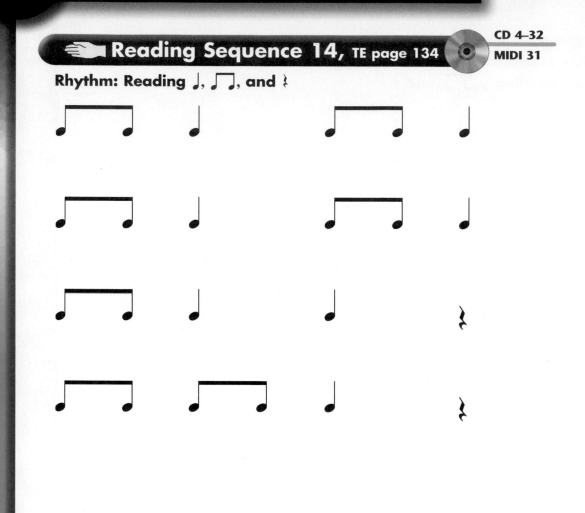

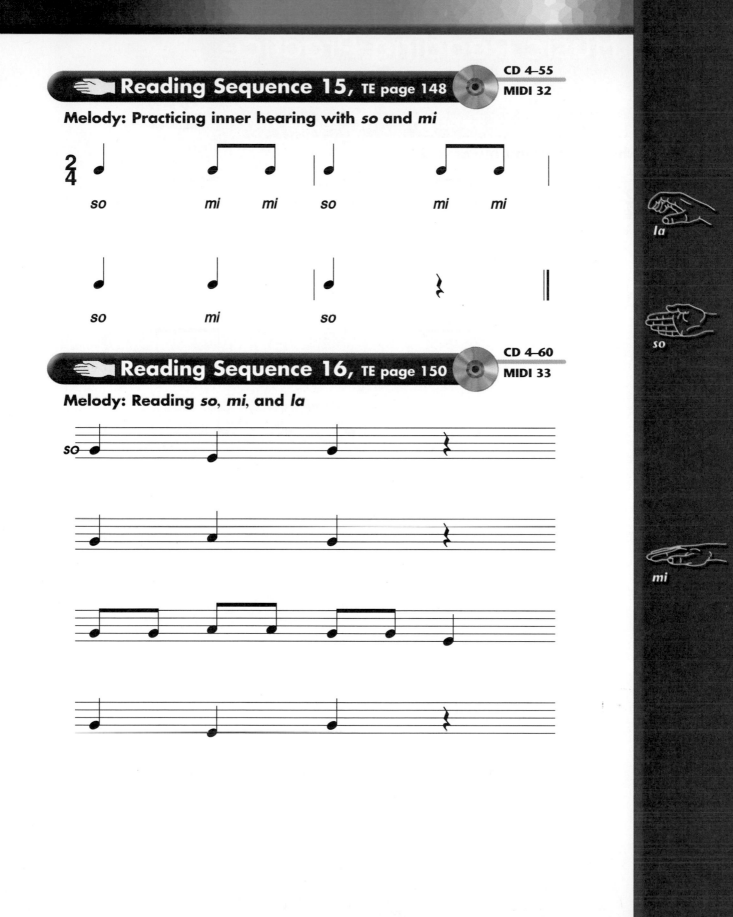

Music Reading Practice

Rhythm: Reading Meter in 2

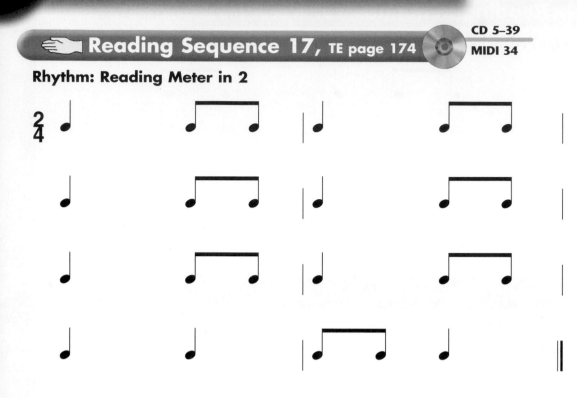

Melody: Reading *so*, *mi*, and *la*

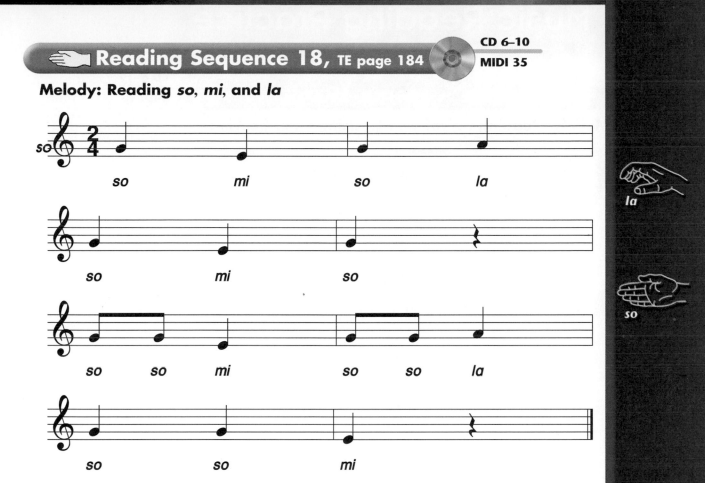

Music Reading Practice

Reading Sequence 19, TE page 188

CD 6–19
MIDI 36

Melody: Reading *so*, *mi*, and *la*, using inner hearing

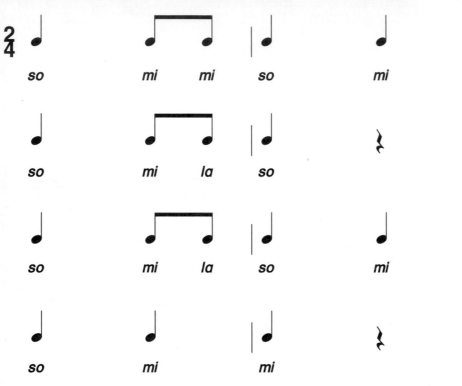

so · mi mi · so · mi

so · mi la so ·

so · mi la so · mi

so · mi · mi ·

Music Reading Practice

Reading Sequence 20, TE page 212

CD 7–3 MIDI 37

Rhythm: Reading ♩, ♫, and 𝄽

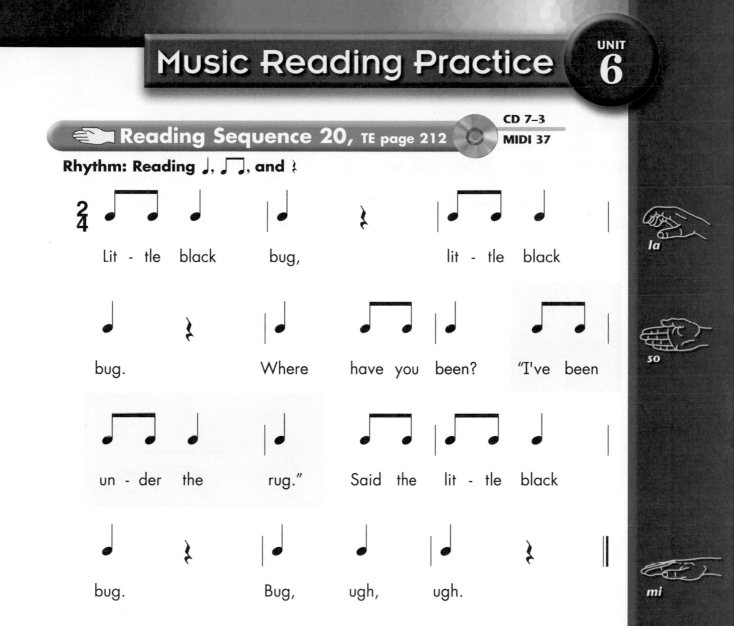

Lit - tle black bug, lit - tle black

bug. Where have you been? "I've been

un - der the rug." Said the lit - tle black

bug. Bug, ugh, ugh.

la

so

mi

CD 7–19
MIDI 38

Reading Sequence 21, TE page 226

Melody: Reading *so*, *mi*, and *la*

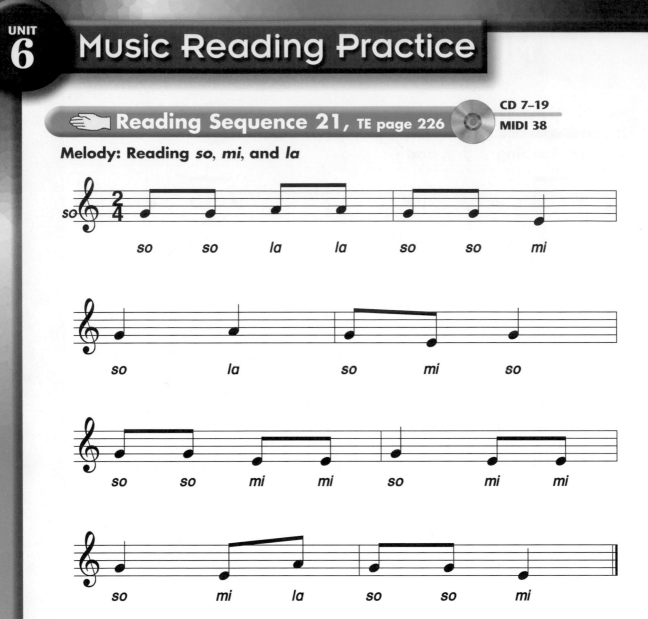

Reading Sequence 22, TE page 228

Melody: Reading *so*, *mi*, *la*, and *do*, using inner hearing

Can You Name This Song?

la

so

mi

do

Mallet Instruments

▲ Xylophone

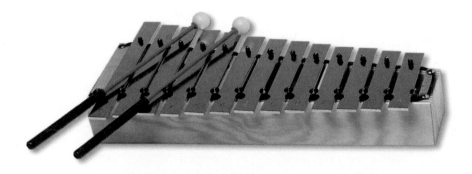

▲ Glockenspiel

Hold the mallets correctly.

Strike the bar in the center.

▼ Alto metallophone

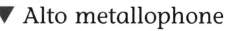

Play this **bordun**.

Sound Bank

 ◀ *Ch'ajch'as*
(dried hoof rattles)

 ▲ *Shekere*

 ▲ Maracas

 ▲ *Guiro*

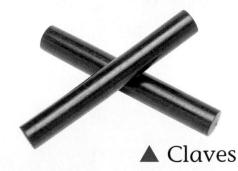 ▲ Claves

Cymbals ▶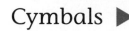

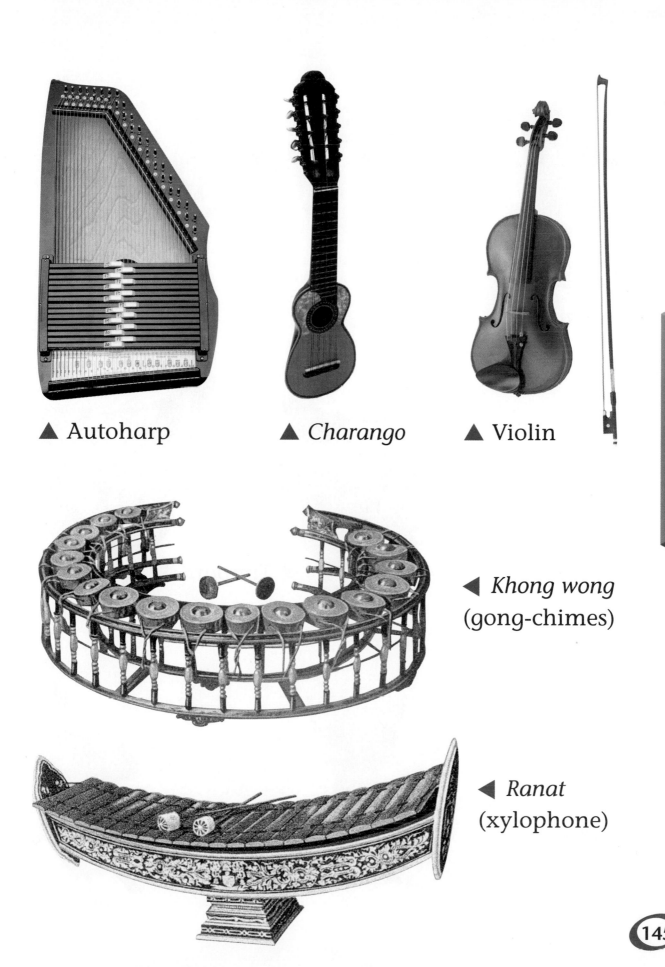

▲ Autoharp

▲ *Charango*

▲ Violin

◀ *Khong wong*
(gong-chimes)

◀ *Ranat*
(xylophone)

▲ *Bombo*

◀ *Tabla*

◀ Timpani ▶

▲ Snare drum

▲ *Djembe*

Taiko drum ▶

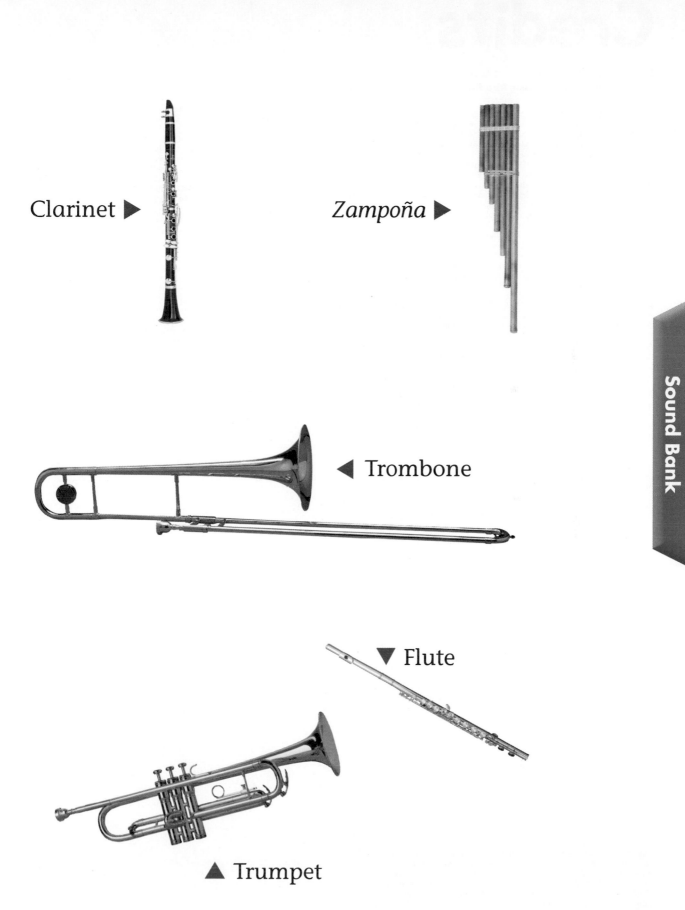

Clarinet ▶

Zampoña ▶

◀ Trombone

▼ Flute

▲ Trumpet

Credits

Design Electronic Production: Kirchoff/Wohlberg, Inc.

Listening Maps and Music Reading Practice: MediaLynx Design Group

Photograph Credits

2: (CL) © Michael St. Maur/Corbis 2: (Bkgd) Jane Burton/© Dorling Kindersley 3: (TC) David W. Hamilton/Getty Images 3: (BC) © Fukuhara, Inc./Corbis 3: (CR) © Lawrence Manning/Corbis 4: © Myrleen Ferguson/PhotoEdit 4: © Nancy Sheehan/PhotoEdit 9: Scala/Art Resource, NY 14: © Peter Weimann/Animals Animals/Earth Scenes 14: Joe McDonald/Animals Animals/Earth Scenes 15: courtesy Arlington National Racecourse 15: © David Stoecklein/The Stock Market 15: © J. & P. Wegner/Animals Animals/Earth Scenes 24: SuperStock 25: Jack Vartoogian 28: © S. Michael Bisceglie/Animals Animals/Earth Scenes 28: Grant Heilman Photography 28: Getty Images 30: John Garrett/© Dorling Kindersley 32: © Richard Hutchings/PhotoEdit 32: SuperStock 35: van Gogh, Vincent. "The Starry Night." (1889) Oil on canvas, 29 x 36 1/4" (73.7 x 92.1 cm). The Museum of Modern Art, New York. Acquired through the Lillie P. Bliss Bequest. Photograph © 2002 The/Museum of Modern Art, New York 36: Jack Vartoogian 36: Dirk R. Franz/Hutchison Library 36: © Crispin Hughes 36: Milt & Joan Mann/Cameramann International, Ltd. 36: © James McCormick/PAL 36: © Crispin Hughes 37: Warren Johnson/Marilyn Rife 40: Staatl. Galerie Moritzburg, Halle/A.K.G., Berlin/SuperStock 42: Milt & Joan Mann/Cameramann International, Ltd. 48: Jan Butchofsky-Houser/Houserstock, Inc. 49: Jack Vartoogian 54: © Dorling Kindersley 55: © Dorling Kindersley 55: Corbis 56 ASAP 60: © Pablo Corral/Corbis 61: © George Holton/Photo Researchers, Inc. 61: Photo © Barry Dawson, from *Traditional Indonesian Textiles* by John Gillow, published by Thames and Hudson Inc., New York 62: Jim Zuckerman/Corbis 65: Kevin Schafer 77: Artville 80: (BCL) © Victoria & Albert Museum, London/Art Resource, NY 82: Getty Images 82: © Rohan/Stone 82: © Maresa Pryor/Animals Animals/Earth Scenes 84: © 97 Ronnie Kaufman/The Stock Market 85: © Dwayne Newton/PhotoEdit 85: © Sotographs/Getty Images 85: © P. DeWilde/Liaison Agency 85: © Stewart Cohen/Stone 87: © Hulton-Deutsch Collection/Corbis 92: © Charles Gupton/Stock Boston 92: © Patrick Ward/Stock Boston 92: © Greg Meadors/Stock Boston 92: Craig Lovell/Corbis 92: © Mike Timo/Stone 92: Corbis 95: Chip and Rosa Maria de la Cueva Peterson 95: Corbis 96: Brenda Joysmith Studio 96: © M. Angelo/Corbis 102: © Don Fawcett/Visuals Unlimited 102: © Breck P. Kent/Animals Animals/Earth Scenes 102: © Rick Poley/Visuals Unlimited 102: Stan Elems/Visuals Unlimited 103: © Patti Murray/Animals Animals/Earth Scenes 103: © Don W. Fawcett/Visuals Unlimited 103: © Patti Murray/Animals Animals/Earth Scenes 103: © Kjell B. Sandved/Visuals Unlimited 103: Zig Leszczynski/Animals Animals/Earth Scenes 106: © Dorling Kindersley 107: From *An Extraordinary Life: The Story of a Monarch Butterfly* by Laurence Pringle, illustrated by Bob Marstall. Illustrations copyright © 1997 by Bob Marstall. Reprinted by permission of Orchard Books, New York. All rights reserved. 109: © Dorling Kindersley 109: © Jack Vartoogian 111: (C) © Luis Castaneda., Inc./Getty Images 111: (CL) Pete Mc Arthur/Getty Images 111: (CR) Andy Crawford/© Dorling Kindersley 117: Bettmann/Corbis-Bettmann 120: (CR) © Robert Frerck/© Robert Frerck/Odyssey/Chicago 120: (BC) Arthur Tilley/Getty Images 121: (B) © David Young-Wolff/PhotoEdit 121: (TC) © Buddy Mays/Corbis

Illustrations

4: Paul Sharp 5: George Thompson 6: George Thompson 8: Jay Johnson 10: Sally Jo Vitsky 11: Michael Morris 12: Michael Morris 14: Dee DeLoy 17: Eileen Mueller Neill 18: Antonio Cangemi 20: Darren McKee 20: Deborah Zemke 21: Darren McKee 22: Deborah Zemke 25: Phyllis Pollema-Cahill 26: Michael Morris 27: Michael Morris 30: Lindy Burnett 32: Lindy Burnett 34: Jim Ishi 36: Paul Sharp 40: Shelly Shinjo 41: Shelly Shinjo 43: Linda Pierce 45: Betsy Day 45: Tony Nuccio 46: Patti Argoff 52: Roman Dunets 57: Phyllis Pollema-Cahill 57: Linda Pierce 58: Elizabeth Wolf 59: Elizabeth Wolf 62: Linda Pierce 63: Linda Pierce 68: David Galchutt 70: Jeffrey Lindberg 72: Higgins Bond 73: Higgins Bond 74: Brent Cottrell 75: Brent Cottrell 76: Patti Argoff 77: Patti Argoff 77: Darren McKee 79: Lynda Calvert Weyant 81: Gail Piazza 82: Margeaux Lucas 86: Darren McKee 88: Carlos Caban 89: Carlos Caban 90: Clive Scruton 91: Clive Scruton 94: Rusty Fletcher 98: Paul Sharp 100: Wayne Parmenter 102: John Wallner 105: Thea Kliros 106: Jay Johnson 109: Linda Pierce 112: Dagmar Fehlav 115: Peter Fasolino 116: Greg Harris

Acknowledgments

5: "Windshield Wipers" from *The Llama Who Had No Pajama: 100 Favorite Poems,* Text copyright © 1974 by Mary Ann Hoberman, reprinted with permission of Harcourt, Inc. Recorded by permission of Gina Maccoby Literary Agency. 6: "Apples, Peaches, Pears, and Plums" (Traditional Children's Rhyme) Rhythmic setting © 2002 Pearson Education, Inc. 21: "Charlie Over the Water" (Traditional Song from the United States) © 2002 Pearson Education, Inc. 29: "Cha yang wu" (Rice Planting Song) (Folk Song from China. English Words © 1988 Silver, Burdett & Ginn, Inc. 41: "Cirmos cica" (Naughty Tabby Cat) (Folk Song from Hungary) English Words © 2002 Pearson Education, Inc. 47: "Bounce High, Bounce Low" (Traditional Game Song from the United States) © 1991 Silver Burdett Ginn. 58: "Snail, Snail', Collected and adapted by Katalin Forrai and Jean Sinor". © 1988 Silver, Burdett & Ginn, Inc." 64: "Little Black Bug" Words by Margaret Wise Brown, Music by Ruth Boshkoff from *All Around the Buttercup,* © 1984 by Schott Music Corp. All Rights Reserved. Used by Permission of European American Music Distributors Corporation, Sole U.S. and Canadian agent for Schott Music Corp. 72: "Mammoth" from *Moon Frog* Text © 1992 Richard Edwards. Illustrations

© 1992 Sarah Fox-Davies. Reproduced by permission of Walker Books Ltd. Published by Candlewick Press, Inc., Cambridge, MA. 76: "The Little Red Hen" © 2002 Pearson Education, Inc. 83: "This Land Is Your Land" Words and Music by Woody Guthrie. TRO © Copyright 1956 (Renewed) 1958 (Renewed) Ludlow Music Publishers, Inc., New York, NY. Used by Permission. 86: "Everybody Says" Words and Music by Malvina Reynolds. Copyright © 1961 Schroder Music Co. (ASCAP); Renewed 1989. Used by Permission. All Rights Reserved. 94: "Banana Splits" Section A: Words by Pat Barnett. Rhythmic setting © 2002 Pearson Education, Inc. Section B: from *Anna Banana: 101 Jump-Rope Rhymes* compiled by Joanna Cole. Text copyright © 1989 by Joanna Cole. Used by Permission of HarperCollins Publishers. 96: "How To Be A Friend" by Pat Lowery Collins, from the book *You and Me,* Orchard Books, 1997. Reprinted by permission. 104: "Beach Rap" © 2002 Pearson Education, Inc. 110: "El Chocolate" (The Chocolate) by José-Luis Orozco, from *De Colores and Other Latin American Folk Songs for Children* by José-Luis Orozco, copyright © 1994 by Jose-Luis Orozco, lyrics and Music arrangements. Used by Permission of Dutton Children's Books, A division of Penguin Young Readers Group, A Member of Penguin Group (USA) Inc., 345 Hudson St., New York, NY 10014. All Rights Reserved. 119: "The End" by A.A. Milne, copyright 1927 by E.P. Dutton, renewed © 1955 by A.A. Milne, from *Now We Are Six* by A.A. Milne. Used by Permission of Dutton Children's Books, a division of Penguin Putnam Inc. Recorded by permission of Curtis Brown Group Ltd., on behalf of the Trustees of the Pooh Properties. 124: "Planting Watermelons" © 2002 Pearson Education, Inc. 124: "Apples" from *A Poem a Day* by Helen H. Moore. Copyright © 1997 by Helen H. Moore. Scholastic Publishing, Inc. 125: "Phoebe" from *Folk Songs of the Southern Appalachians.* Collected by Cecil J. Sharp and Edited by Maud Karpeles. © Oxford University Press 1932. 127: "Bee, Bee Bumblebee" Rhythmic setting © 2002 Pearson Education, Inc. 128: "Charlie Over the Water" © 2002 Pearson Education, Inc. 132: "Cuckoo, Cuckoo" © 1983 Silver Burdett Company. 135: "Bounce High, Bounce Low" © 1991 Silver Burdett Ginn. 139: "Little Black Bug" Words by Margaret Wise Brown, Music by Ruth Boshkoff from *All Around the Buttercup,* © 1984 by Schott Music Corp. 140: "Johnny Caught a Flea" from *The Kodaly Method,* 2E by Lois Choksy, © 1989. Prentice-Hall, Inc., Upper Saddle River, NJ.

Index of Songs

and Speech Pieces